SUPER BLOOD WOLF MOON

SUPER BLOOD WOLF MOON
Copyright © Gary V. Powell 2020
All Rights Reserved
Published by Kallisto Gaia Press Inc.
Printed in the United States of America
First Edition

No part of this book may be used or reproduced in any manner whatsoever without written permission except in the case of brief quotations embodied in critical articles or reviews.

Attention schools and businesses: for discounted copies on large orders please contact the publisher directly.

Kallisto Gaia Press Inc.
1801 E. 51st Street
Suite 365-246
Austin TX 78723
Phone: (254) 654-7205
www.kallistogaiapress.org

Cover Design: Tony Burnett
Cover Photo: Gary V. Powell
Editor: Tony Burnett

ISBN: 978-1-952224-01-0

SUPER BLOOD WOLF MOON

POEMS

GARY V. POWELL

DEDICATION

This chapbook is dedicated to my best friend, constant muse, and loving wife, the irrepressible Mary K. Wilson.

Contents

On Learning of the Death of an Old Girlfriend on Facebook before Finishing Your First Cup of Coffee	1
Corporate Warriors	3
Snakebite	5
I-77 Viaduct	6
Our Thoughts and Prayers	7
When I'm Ninety-Five	9
T-Boned Sestina	11
Crowder Peas	13
The Night the Condom Broke	14
Opioid Crisis	17
Milwaukee	18
The Old Main Drag	20
Basic Training	21
Super Blood Wolf Moon	23
Cheating Hearts	26
Black Tar Night	28
Algorithm	29
When Wifey's Away	32
White	33
Dormers	35
South Beach (in Iambic Pentameter) with a Nod to Stuart Dybek	37
Cable Line Road	38
How to Make a Garden	40
Acknowledgements	43

On Learning of the Death of an Old Girlfriend on Facebook before Finishing Your First Cup of Coffee

When your old girlfriends
begin to die like
dogs you've buried over
the years,

and it's a rainy Monday
morning, the first Monday
morning following springing
forward so we can save the light,

but there's no light
to save this morning, no sun
to penetrate, and it's hard
to move much less spring,

when your old girlfriends
begin to die like
cars you've owned and traded
in over the years,

and you take your current
dogs for their morning
walk in the spring rain
falling from a dark sky,

but they'll never be the dogs
that black and white Springer was,
whose ashes now reside on the book
shelf next to which you like to write,

when your old girlfriends
begin to die like
moths flattened to the wall,
shadows from the night before,

and you think while walking the dogs
in the dark and the rain
what a beautiful girl was
blonde and blue-eyed Lizbeth Fontaine,

but just a little freaky even then,
those hippie-dippie days
of sex, drugs, and the scent of
napalm in the good morning starshine,

when your old girlfriends
begin to die like annual
flowers planted with
such hope every spring,

and those adolescent breasts
swimming braless beneath
a tie-dyed t-shirt in the backseat
of daddy's cherry red Camaro,

but also the tiny barefoot
dancer on the Camaro's hood,
shim, shim, shimmying
to the sound of your air guitar,

when your old girlfriends
begin to die like
wine bottles emptied on the screen
porch and recycled in the bin,

and kiss kiss kissing
those starry-starry nights away,
your very own Lucy in the sky
in the sum sum summer of love,

when your old girlfriends
begin to die like
rushing rivulets of rain
disappearing down a sewage drain.

Corporate Warriors

Remember when we were profiles
in likeness in our gray business
attire, splash of color in our ties,
cell phone whining in our ears.

We had important places to be
as we careened through streets
and airports, teleconferenced
with peers, interfaced and met.

We did it for our families, our companies
and our teams, for the false sense of
security that allowed us to sleep through
the night. For the sweet suck of the deal.

We queued up at our cubicles, genuflected
and crossed ourselves before the throne
of the corporate prophet, awaiting the
news: merger, acquisition, or divestiture.

And in the CEO's name we prayed:

"This stock option is my body
Think of me when you eat.
This red ink is my blood
Think of me when you drink."

Remember when we were gray men,
hollow women, living in a dead
land, a land stuffed with IOUs
and motherfucking lawyers.

We were the in-between, the rut
and rub on the road from desire
to spasm. We were the gut wrench
of the downward trending Dow.

So:

"Thanks for the daily bread, man,
and forgive us our debts, although we
we will never forgive our debtors. For

shareholder value is the kingdom and the power and the glory and the stick with which we beat the competition into submission."

SNAKEBITE

Dreamed last night of snakes
in my bed, crawling out of my new
mattress, slithering through my sheets,
and snuggling between my legs,

probably because I relented and
granted my pimply, seventeen-year-old
permission to join the Army—early,
like the moment he graduates high school—

instead of safely attending college
like middle-class white boys are
supposed to do, like we always
hoped and expected he would.

At least he has a purpose and goals
other than lying around the house,
slacking off, and playing video games,
but his purpose is to avoid exams,

and his goals are to leap from airplanes,
blow shit up, and kill bad guys, and I've never
done any of that and was prepared in my day to
flee to Canada rather than put myself in harm's way
or kill another human being just so some politician
could save face or get re-elected.

Yeah, burn, baby, burn.

The snakes were copperheads,
probably because I nearly
stepped on one while walking
the park the other day.

Probably kill you, or maybe not,
if a Good Samaritan rushes you
to Urgent Care in the nick of
time, but the alligators.

They also populate my dreams
and are something else. They'll
kill you for sure, and if the 'gators
don't get you, T-Rex will.

I-77 Viaduct

He once threw his wife
out the door of his Honda
Accord at the light this side
of the Highway 77 viaduct,

like twenty years ago, like
five years into a marriage
that felt in those days as
fragile as a single note
plucked on his old guitar.

She said something unkind
or at least something
he perceived as unkind, and
the bright sunlight and blue
sky of that hot summer's
day conspired to blind him
to less violent choices, besides
which, she *wanted* out of the car.
.
Or maybe, it was on the other side
of the viauct where they argued,
at the farmer's market over okra or
scones or flowers or some slight,
or perceived slight, committed
by him, like admiring another
woman's breasts or behind, and
she told *him* to take a hike.

In those days they were
two pieces of sand paper
rubbing each other raw
with loathing and desire.

These days they're more like pillows
comforting one another on a worn
and familiar sofa than knives
threatening or sparks flying
or glass splintering
into bare skin.

Our Thoughts and Prayers

This is the bullet
inscribed with your name
and the cartridge box
where it resides
beside
nine-hundred
and ninety-nine
siblings.

This is a two-twenty-three
Remington round
designed with
brass casing,
boxer priming,
boat-tailing
and full metal jacket,
for accuracy
and range.

At fifty-five grain,
this bullet is light
but powerful
with a muzzle velocity
of three thousand
feet per second
and energy measured
at twelve hundred
foot-pounds.

This is an AR-15,
chambered and hungry,
a rifle
that when fully loaded
is poised to enjoy
the meal it deserves,
not a mere snack,
but a banquet.

This is the name
of your malaise—
a thousand rounds
when one will do—
and a beast
that feeds
without remorse
even when its belly
is full.

This is the sound
of flesh torn,
bones shattered,
and organs exploded,
the scent
of exposed viscera,
and the color
of blood.

This is the bullet
inscribed with your name
and the hot summer's path
it took
through walls
and glass
and alley ways
to find you,
friend.

When I'm Ninety-Five

Stacy had a heart attack,
at home, she explained on the
tennis court today. Granted,
she's overweight, lives alone,
except for her cats, prefers mimosas
to coffee, eggs benedict to bagels and
lox, and cigarettes to reefer.

But still, she's only mid-fifties, about
my wife's age, the woman I married
when she was barely twenty-seven
and I was pushing forty-two, and
everyone laughed we wouldn't last. Well,
now, I'm sixty-eight and sometimes
my heart aches, too. Sometimes, I get dizzy
when the earth spins like a bitch
beneath my feet, not to mention
the cataracts, bad knees, and
underactive thyroid.

But who am I to complain? My wife,
my beautiful, young wife had a stroke in
her eye, a fucking stroke in her eye, a
capillary that burst like a super nova
in some distant galaxy, and almost
left us with a black hole. Due to workplace
stress, the doc said, so now, once a month
she gets a shot right here, right here in her
right eye, so she won't go blind. I hold her
hand and distract her with bullshit
about my day—writing at Starbucks and
walking the dogs—and then, afterwards,
we make love because while you
can, you damn sure should.

At least we've seen Paris in spring
and Dublin in summer, saved my daughter
from suicide, hiked the Great Divide,
driven to Ensenada in the rain,
and watched my mother die. We've won
our share of mixed doubles matches,
walked San Francisco in the fog,

run naked on the beach at Big Sur,
and had our fortunes told on Bourbon Street.

Stacy knew heart attack
because that elephant you always hear
about crossed her manicured lawn, pushed
Mac the Cat off her lap, and sat on her
chest for what seemed a very long time,
bursting a cholesterol sack and blocking
arterial blood flow, causing her to lose
breath and see life pass before her
just like they say it does.

But she remained cool
as that cucumber you always hear
about, fed the cats, brushed her teeth, and
called 911, the paramedics advising one
more minute and she'd have been dead as
Marilyn Monroe, who Stacy thinks she resembled
in her younger days, men falling at her feet
like leaves from her Japanese Maple
on a cloudy, autumn day.

Anyway, she's back on-court
with that crappy backhand and
flat forehand that couldn't put away
Rusty Knox even before he underwent hip
surgery. But she's out here, goddammit, and
I'm glad she is because when I'm ninety-five,
my girl will be eighty-one, and even if we can't
drink wine on the screen porch by twinkle
light while listening to Robert Earl Keen
sing about how the road goes on forever
and the party never ends, due to failing livers
or kidneys, or make love standing on our heads
like that couple on Saint Lucia claimed they could
and even offered to show us how for a thousand
America dollars, I hope we'll still snuggle like
teenagers on Momma's couch because
while you can, you damn sure should.

T-Boned Sestina

To the young woman who T-boned
my Infiniti sedan while texting
in her Ford 150 as she roared
up a rain-danced entrance ramp
like a Texas tornado or Amarillo
cowboy sporting his nine-inch rodeo

or an Austin cowgirl enjoying her first rodeo.
To the woman who hard-crash T-boned
our lives together, far south of Amarillo,
her eyes on his hoss, sexting, texting,
her pedal to the metal up that ramp,
her pride in the wind as she roared

into my passenger-side door, roared
like a bull out the gate of his first rodeo,
like a gunfighter's bullet shot off that ramp,
her Juicy-Lucy cyber innuendoes T-boned
to an iPhone's screen, sexting, texting
her concupiscent cowboy in Amarillo.

Oh, when the wind don't blow in Amarillo.
Oh, when white freightliners roared
across East Texas years before texting
threatened drivers with their last ro-de…oh,
just two more inches would have T-boned
me clean to eternity on that Mo-Pac ramp.

But li'l darlin', all of life is but an exit ramp
off the lost highway to windy Amarillo
or any other cow town, and one might be T-boned
by lightning as easily as the hormones that roared
in your tight-fitting jeans like a pro-circuit rodeo
that wild-west Texas morning while texting

love or lust, dumb-luck thumbs texting
life, slow like sludge down a ramp,
death, fast as an unbroken mustang rodeo,
life, ticking like a 3 AM clock that roared,
death, like armadillo roadkill T-boned
on that dusty trail to panhandle Amarillo.

See, the buckety-buck of the rodeo is the humpety-hump of texting, a beefsteak, bloody and T-boned, grins at the end of every ramp, and a lanky caballero in Amarillo sent the dick-pic that roared.

Crowder Peas

Remembered picking crowder peas
for the first time in years.

Dreamed about a girl I hadn't seen
since her father passed away.

Was reminded by a lilac's scent
of a garden I once tilled.

All this, walking down a street
I hardly know, surrounded by
people whose acquaintance
I'll likely never make.

Saw in a spider's web the doilies
my grandma would crochet.

Heard in a dog's plaintive bark
the Husky on my father's farm.

Remembered picking crowder peas
for the first time in years.

THE NIGHT THE CONDOM BROKE

I was twenty-one and you were twenty, and we
were fighting so much we decided to break up.

You were already seeing someone else,
a business student with better prospects.

And I was dropping out of school and leaving
for LA to find myself and maybe write a novel.

I nearly wrecked your car driving home from the bar
where we'd gone to say goodbye and drink margaritas.

You claimed I did it on purpose, to make a
point, but in fact I'd swerved to avoid a deer.

I said you were too immature for real love, and
you said if you were immature, then what was I.

I said it wasn't too late for you to change
your mind and accompany me to LA.

And you said if I'd wanted your company in
LA, I should've let on sooner rather than later.

And I said fuck it, and you said that's what
I always said when things didn't go my way.

When we arrived at my apartment, I asked
you to come inside and you said no thanks.

But then changed your mind because you needed
to pee and preferred my toilet to the parking lot.

My roommate gone for the weekend, we
were alone except for his damn gerbils.

You left the door open and I sat in the
dark and listened to your familiar tinkle.

Then I started to cry, and when you sat next
to me on the sofa, you started crying, too.

After we finished crying, you said you'd like to do
it one last time, so we'd have that to remember.

And I said that would be nice because
I didn't want to remember us like this.

In the past, even when our verbal assaults
had been brutal, our lovemaking was tender.

But that night our kisses were rough enough to bruise,
and when I pinched, you said pinch harder, bitch.

And then you bit my neck and held on, sucking
and leaving a bluish, purple two-week hickey.

I slid a hand between your legs and searched
like a man fingering seat cushions for spare change.

You moaned oh my god, oh my god and thrust
your hips and pelvis like a piston in a sleeve.

I kicked off my shoes while you unbuckled
my belt and tugged at my zipper.

You tore off my favorite flannel shirt, sending
buttons tap-dancing across a linoleum floor.

I pushed you away when you offered your mouth
because I refused to settle for less than your soul.

So, you bent double across the sofa's arm, your favorite
position, and ordered me to put it in already, goddammit.

So, I ripped off the condom wrapper and you
helped with the condom before guiding me home.

And then we bucked hard and fast until it was over,
lickety-split, leaving both of us spent and embarrassed.

Because we'd never done it quite like that before, rutting
like a stallion and his mare in some dappled meadow.

Embarrassed because this was the *last* time, and it was
this time we'd be left with as we went our separate ways.

Then lying side by side, left to contemplate our lust and
passion and swim in our separate puddles of bodily fluid,

You said did that mother break?
And I said kinda looks that way.

And you said don't you even know how
to put a condom on for christssake?

Plus, I think you knocked over the gerbil
cage, and I said no, I think you did.

And you said you were super regular,
which meant you were ovulating that week.

And I joked we'd better hope my sperm were more like
floaters down the lazy river than barbarians at the city's gate.

And you asked if I was ever going to grow up,
and I said fuck it because that's what I always said.

And you said this was great, just great,
and I said you could say that again.

Opioid Crisis

When your dealer doesn't show.

When your lover steals your stash.

When the doc won't write your script.

When the pain rages like the day your dog died.

When the leg you lost
chases you around
the house
like a terrorist
who grew up
in a refugee camp
that smells
like the toilet
you can't flush
because you forgot
to pay
the fucking
water bill.

MILWAUKEE

In Milwaukee, snow choked the roads first of
December and continued to fall through end of
April, burying hopes for an early spring and
piling higher than the locals' sock-capped heads.

In Milwaukee, the breeze on the bridge that traveled to
nowhere, the bridge like a tree cut off at the knees,
sometimes smelled as sweet as the pinewoods up
north where everyone went to hunt deer in autumn.

In Milwaukee, you lived down the hall in a small
apartment that faced a dreary parking lot and were
content with that until I introduced you to my view
of Canada geese who applauded every rising sun.

In Milwaukee, a water fountain was a bubbler,
and a traffic light a stop-and-go, and co-workers
didn't lend us money, they borrowed it to us, instead,
and Friday fish fries were always all we could eat.

In Milwaukee, the adjacent great lake lay flat
and gray as a death shroud or dazzled like shards
of broken glass across an abandoned factory's floor
or palmed the harvest moon like a giant smiley face.

In Milwaukee, I deemed you an apple heiress because
your modest and hard-working family owned orchards,
and your father deemed me a red-blooded American boy
even though I was neither Lutheran nor of German descent.

In Milwaukee, they made life insurance and motorcycles,
put on lake front festivals, and cheered for the Pack
and the Bucks and the Brewers while slamming brats
and swilling a couple-two-or-three cold beers.

In Milwaukee, young folks married in churches and held
receptions in bowling alleys, preferring polka over soft
rock and pot luck potato salad, Jell-O Delight, sausages,
cheese curds, and home-smoked salmon over catered cuisine.

In Milwaukee, I practiced law and you drew blood. We
bought houses and cars and started a family. We vacationed
in Florida in winter and in summer your family's lake cottage
where the water was freezing and the mosquitos savage.

In Milwaukee, people were friendly and progressive,
believing in unions and sharing the wealth so long as
the Darkies stayed to the west and the Spics to the south,
and the Welfare Mammies didn't move up from Chicago.

In Milwaukee, the breeze on the bridge that traveled to
nowhere, like a man cut off at the knees, sometimes
smelled rank as rotten eggs when the wind blew in
from Gary's steel mills or Kenosha's rendering plant.

In Milwaukee, we learned we were not meant for one
another, growing apart while refusing to own it until
forced to own it, due, I suppose, to all we'd bought
and started, and the weight of our great big mistake.

THE OLD MAIN DRAG

The old main drag,
pool hall to turn around,
is forever and ever lean,
mean, and seventeen.

The old main drag,
gasoline and perfume,
is a blue-eyed blonde
in a rag-top 'Vette, 1962.

The old main drag,
railroad to river,
is a cheeseburger, fries,
and a malted chocolate shake.

The old main drag,
cigarettes and reefer,
is a bare-knuckle brawl
and a busted upper lip.

The old main drag,
Marion street to Beardsley,
is her hand on your thigh
and her tongue in your ear.

The old main drag,
cold beer and Naugahyde,
is Cassady and Kerouac,
and you ain't never going back.

The old main drag,
post office to liquor store,
is Saturday night
never going to end.

The old main drag,
cars muscled to the line,
is school boys pissing
lusty in a prairie wind.

Basic Training

Yes, Drill Sergeant, Yes!

In you we trust to re-make our babies,
reengineer slack bodies
into jagged granite cliffs breaking steep against the sea,
reconfigure puppy-dog hearts
into clockwork machines,
and transform inquiring minds into reptilian brains.

Yes, Drill Sergeant, Yes!

For young men and women are meant
to be broken like wild horses,
their free and nascent spirits driven
from budding adolescent flesh, so that in the end
we're left with diamond-hard nuggets
fit only for the tips of ambitious politicians' spears.

Yes, Drill Sergeant, Yes!

And tender souls are meant to be rendered
like fat from bacon in the fry pan,
leaving bits as sere and crisp as the breezes
that whip ice crystals over distant mountain tops
or swirl across ancient desert dunes soaked
in crude oil and the blood of holy martyrs.

Yes, Drill Sergeant, Yes!

They must turn away from their mothers
and fathers their once smooth and smiling faces,
now become the cruel masks of killers
skilled in the way of the gun and the knife.
They must unclasp their once soft hands
now become clubs with which to pummel.

Yes, Drill Sergeant, Yes!

For their destiny is to arrive in the night
by stealth and with violence,
kicking down doors, slaughtering baying dogs,
and casting wives and babes aside

before delivering the double tap of death and collecting their fallen enemy's DNA.

Yes, Drill Sergeant, Yes!

Super Blood Wolf Moon

Retired, now, like a hardy geranium that
refuses to bloom in winter, you

walk the familiar path beside Lake
Norman this cold January

morning because you have the
time, now, to do what

you want, now, when you
want, like the old dog

that trots behind, now,
but mostly wastes

his days lying on the sofa.

You've seen this first, full winter moon before,
hanging like a lantern over Indiana corn fields,

floating like a Mardi Gras mask over Lake
Ponchartrain, rising like a New Year's

ball over Lake Michigan, and riding
like a horseman over Iowa prairie.

But here it is again, tinted pink
by the sunrise over your

shoulder, sinking behind
the southern pine,

casting a sheen across
the cold water

that sloshes against the stones at your feet.

You've seen a lot because you're retired, now,
like the winter copperheads burrowed beneath

these stones, and you have plenty of time,
now, to contemplate this moon, cool,

indifferent witness to cataclysmic
cosmic events beyond your

reckoning. They call it "super"
because during this phase it

leans nearest the earth and
appears larger than

usual, revealing its
blemishes like

scars etched on the old dog's belly.

They call it "bloody" not because this is the
time for transfusing or drawing blood

or testing for disease or genomic
flaws that guarantee early

memory loss or heart failure,
but because when the

earth eclipses the moon,
like time eclipsing

that old dog, trotting
behind you, now,

the sun casts
its shadow,

burnishing ancient and aging craters.

They call it "wolf," this first full moon of the
new year, because this is the season when

coyotes mate and wolves howl with
hunger, when brittle branches

snap in the wake of your passing,
when the old dog's breath

fogs like steam rising from newly
dug graves, when despite

the cold and solitude
you decide to sit

awhile, now, before
heading home

because you and the old dog are tired, now.

CHEATING HEARTS

Sunday mornings
saw my mother to
church, chiffon dresses
and high-heeled shoes.

While she lobbied our souls'
salvation, life everlasting and
a place before the Throne, my father
stayed home and played his stereo.

George Jones and Eddy Arnold,
Ray Price and Ernest Tubb, walked
his floors and danced honky-tonk
angels through neon nights.

Hank Snow drove ninety miles
an hour down a dead-end street,
and Whisperin' Bill Anderson
held love on the tips of his fingers.

Roy, Dale, and Trigger rode
happy trails across our carpet
while Marty Robbins loved
Wicked Felina and died for her sins.

Jesus saved, but Jim Beam
walked us through our troubles
and cast his warm amber light
on a wilder side of life.

The Beast pawed and snorted
outside our door, threatening
eternal flame, while Kitty Wells
played guitar and sang "Make-Believe."

How high's the water, Momma?
High enough to wash us clean.
How high's the water, Daddy?
Five   foot   high   and   risin'.

*Wide is the gate and broad is
the road that leads to destruction,
but small is the gate and narrow
the road that leads to life.*

Yet, judge not, lest ye be judged,
for how many of you have heard
that lonesome whippoorwill sing
or walked the streets of Bakersfield?

BLACK TAR NIGHT

Somewhere a needle
searches for a vein
that hasn't collapsed

like a flat tire on a
lonely country road,
leaving you stranded

next to a farmhouse
occupied by a guy
who kills for relief

from the voices in
his head and the
demons in his gut

and sews the skin of
his victims onto the
seat of his easy chair.

Algorithm

If this, then that, until the problem solved…

If this, then that, starting with The Big Bang,
explaining each particle, planet, star, and
galaxy, each black hole and vast expanse
of dark matter, dark energy, and antimatter,
in between,
predicting the rate of expansion and collapse,
quantifying the potential for uncertainty in
prediction, and estimating the many
multiverses in which you exist
or not.

If this, then that…

If you Google cheeseburger, then you
might enjoy a Big Mac or Hardee's Bacon
Stuffed Gut Buster Deluxe, or a cashmere
sweater and leather driving gloves from
Banana Republic,
to keep you warm while driving around
in search of your perfect cheeseburger,
or maybe you need to lower cholesterol
and blood pressure, so how about trying
MDs Online.

If this, then that...

If you search for fire wood, then you
might need Viagra or Cialis, or perhaps
Best Briefs for Men, designed to make
you appear fitter and better display
your wood,
or could it be that hardwood cabinets
on sale from Lowes are what you
really need, in fact, a complete
kitchen makeover with appliances you
can't afford.

If this, then that...

If you lose your job with Mega-bank,
allowing officers and shareholders
to pay themselves larger salaries and
dividends, then how about yoga
or meditation,
or that AK-47 you've been
Jonesin' for, so you can gun
down the bank's CEO with the
bullet that bears his, her, or
their name.

If this, then that...

If your wife dumps you for a younger man,
you probably have it coming because this
is the natural consequence of robbing the
cradle of a twenty-something when you were
forty-something,
or if your son joins the Army so he can
leap from airplanes and kill bad guys,
you probably have it coming, because you
were once a war protesting, dope-smoking
hippie dude.

If this, then that…

If dinosaurs were really mammals instead
of soulless, bone crushing or tree eating
reptiles, then it's understandable why the
petroleum jelly they became is so worth
fighting for,
and why the vast seas of their remains bubble
beneath oceans of sand over which Saudi princes
rule, enjoying the riches of their pollution—
sulfur dioxide and nitrogen oxide—while polar
ice melts.

If this, then that…

If a butterfly flaps its wings, then ancient
forests will fall and even species heretofore
unidentified become extinct, whales cease
to ply the seas, and bees refuse their calling
to pollinate,
and if only one child goes to bed hungry tonight,
or only one tear falls to earth today, or only one
heart breaks like the San Andreas fault
this year, then ask for no more
next year.

When Wifey's Away

I dance naked on the porch
while singing "Walking the Floor."

I eat tuna from a can and
mayo from a Mason jar.

I read the Book of Mormon while
watching Internet porn.

I snuggle with my pillow and
spoon my guitar.

I bowl with the dogs and
shoot craps with the cats.

I pick nits with the carpet and
a fight with the fridge.

I learn to speak Russian
and how to build a bridge.

I attend Presidential rallies
before dropping Twitter turds.

I practice saying "I love you,"
so I won't forget the words.

White

Sometimes, I feel as white as the
rice they once raised on plantations
upriver and floated on barges down
to Charleston and Savannah,

like that morning, three years past on
Shellman's Bluff, overlooking the rising tide,
the river, and the salt marsh. A blood-orange
sun ascending a Confederate-gray sky,

snapping turtles and crappie fighting
over my bait, and my Georgia-boy
fishing guide jawing about the slave
ship they found on Blackbeard's Island:

*"Say, maybe you don't know, but if we
hadn't made slaves of 'em, they'd
have enslaved themselves or killed
each other or been eaten by lions.*

*"And, now, some Atlanta politician, a'
course she's black, wants me to pay
reparations and support affirmative
action so more of 'em can go to college.*

*"But what about my kids, nary a one
went to college, so where's my white
privilege, know what I'm sayin'? Anyways,
that's a good lookin' fish, you caught, son.*

*"Take it down to Hunter's where that
black gal will cook it up for you
real good—don't get me wrong
a'cause I'm not racist, or anything."*

Sometimes, I feel as white as
the belly of that crappie, caught
on that salt-marsh morning,
Shellman's Bluff, spring 2016.

Sometimes, I feel as white
as the Aryan light that illuminated
the path to the gas chambers
of Auschwitz and Buchenwald.

Sometimes, I feel as white as the
snow fallen on native mountain ranges,
long since stolen and carved into
sandstone and tar-paper reservations.

Sometimes, I feel so white that
sunlight passes through, so white
and slick that nothing sticks,
so white I'm the fog that blinds

DORMERS

You pay four hundred
cash for a job no one wants
and doubt from the get-go
Joe is up to the task.

But he's cheaper than the rest,
has cleaned your gutters
five years straight and says
man, I appreciate.

Says him and the little
woman, married twenty years,
are on the outs, fighting over
the house, dogs, and custody.

She's kicked him to the
curb, and now it's down
to a pallet on his sister's floor
and a lawyer he can't afford.

He's a skinny sack of bones,
a tweaker's split-toothed grin
beneath a baseball cap,
jeans cut off at the knees.

So, you hand over the cash,
wondering how it was in the
beginning for him and his
woman when their love was new
and fresh as a sailor's first shore
leave and their kisses lingered
on Momma's porch swing and love
snaked their hearts like morning glory,

wondering what got between
their lips and the tendrils,
leaving them rusty with dust
and eaten by weeds,
knowing all along that such
matters as these more resemble
a puzzle with missing pieces than
a carpenter's level or painter's edge.

We're talking third-story dormers
on a house that floats high
above the street like a
thunderhead on the horizon.

There's likely rot in those crevices,
caulking required before paint applied.
Maybe not every little thing
can be fixed for the least price.

Joe clinches the bills, saying
it's two hundred to start
and the rest for supplies, and
then you never see him again.

Maybe blows your cash on meth
before even reaching Lowes,
maybe loses his courage to your
roof's pitch and the long way down.

Maybe accepts a better offer
or plans to paint your
dormers another day until one
day melts into the next and the
next and the next and he just lets go,
lets go of his wife, lawyer, kids, truck,
and life in general. No one's walked
the dark side of his moon.

The next man has a crew,
shiny trucks and new ladders,
and wants twenty-five hundred,
five hundred up front.

They arrive on time and
finish before the day is through,
leaving you to ponder further
tender mysteries.

Like how is it that when
you kiss your own wife of twenty
years, her brown eyes remain the
only abyss you've ever fallen into?

South Beach (in Iambic Pentameter) with a Nod to Stuart Dybek

We did not wear thongs or Speedos
in hope of exposing ass cheeks or penises
to strangers as we made our way to the beach.

We did not strike muscle poses
designed to advertise our exquisite bodies
to modeling agencies seeking talent.

We did not eschew suntan lotion
in favor of baby oil, thus burning
our white Yankee faces cancerous red.

We did not lose our expensive bling
to the sand and the fat old men
hoovering for treasure with metal detectors.

We did not allow our black dogs to run
unleashed, frightening children and grandmas,
and pooping and pissing wherever they wished.

We did not drink mojitos until
we puked broad daylight into the Atlantic's
on-rushing waves, spring break breasts heaving free.

We did not dry hump to mind-shattering
orgasms under our thin blue blanket
while under-age boys pointed and giggled.

No, South Beach, no, Miami, we never.

CABLE LINE ROAD

Because you are fifteen and greedy
for experience and want to show
the adult world you are poised
to join the fray, saying
hey, look at me now, two in the morning,
three below zero, snow and ice piled
high as Jimi Hendrix or Janis Joplin, a
dubious moon wishing on an unsure star.

Oh, aren't you cool, sneaky-
Pete out the window, down the
way to where Jerry waits in the
lane in his daddy's sixty-eight Nova,
smoke from your Marlboro curling like
a serpent overhead because you are a man,
a real man, just look at the wispy tendrils
trying out your Steve McQueen upper lip.

Isn't that what Vicki said, you reminded
her of Steve McQueen, with your blue eyes
and sandy hair, your tight-jean swagger
and *faux* leather jacket, all you could afford?

So, ride in the souped-up Super Nova out to
the cable line road, underage and underbuilt,
Jagger and "No Satisfaction" booming on the
eight-track. *No one smokes the same cigarette as you.*

The cable line road where so many wanna-be
Steve McQueens have already marked the
quarter mile, Stickle's farm to Detwiler's barn,
with rubber and blood, rubber and blood.

Egg your friend on with ain't nothin' worth
nothin' except it's free, man, the times they are
a changin', man, and like they say,
no one gets outta here alive, anyway, man.

Incite Ole Jer to rev the engine, a fuel-injected
three ninety-six overhead cam with four
on the floor, tell him to pop the fucking clutch
already and bring the g-force press to your chest.

Then hit a patch of black ice that's waited
for you since before you were born,
spin out and roll that baby, two, three times,
total the Nova in an Indiana corn field.

See, there is a time for everything,
a time for every season and reason,
Hendrix and Janis, Morrison and
McQueen, *turn, turn, turn.*

But this is not your time, even
if you might wish it so, for your time
is yet to come, marked on a calendar and
locked in a vault to which you lack access.

With that full moon grinning down on
you, fool, crawl out a broken window, assess
the sprained ankle, bloodied scalp, and busted
lip, then limp three miles home.

Along the cable line road,
you and ole Jer, chins out, arms
locked in the grip of an arctic high
blown in on the heels of an Alberta Clipper.

How to Make a Garden

This is how you make a garden.

Clear a space, a space in the sun,
of trees and bushes, vines and thorn,
as you might carve your torpid heart from
your chest and lift it into the light, so that the
hard-earned scars may heal, and it beats wild again.

This is how you make a garden.

Till the space by hand, or with a power tiller,
if you're able to bear the noise, turning the soil,
as you might cultivate your fallow mind to converse
with mountains, trees, and valleys, with fish of the sea,
birds of the sky, beasts of the land, and worms of the earth.

This is how you make a garden.

Plant the clear space with seeds and starts
of beans and peppers, tomatoes and zucchini,
as you might fill your mouth with and break your
teeth on exotic fare from foreign lands, so that by taste
and texture you are satisfied, and the stranger is embraced.

This is how you make a garden.

Water your seeds and starts when no
rain falls and fertilize if the soil is poor,
as you might lie with a lover, caressing her
breasts and belly and scenting her scent, so that
in the end she inherits your debt and also your wealth

This is how you make a garden.

Tend your plants by teasing choking weeds
from emerging growth with a sharp-edged hoe,
as you might guide a lost or hopeless child across
the star-soaked sky, into galaxies of possibility, granting
her exploding super nova radiation through space and time.

This is how you make a garden.

Pick your produce as it ripens. Eat it now or can
and put it up in the pantry to enjoy on a winter's day,
as you might hold close the best memories of your life,
whether real or imagined, true or false, so that they sustain
through old age, physical illness, and other times of trepidation.

This is how you make a garden.

Collect and remove the wilted stalks and
blackened leaves deadened by fall's first frost,
as you might dispose of the corpses left by drought,
famine, disease, and war, so that only the abandoned
land and whispering wind bear witness to the holocaust.

This is how you make a garden.

Carve your torpid heart from your chest and raise it to the light.
Cultivate your mind to converse with mountains and trees.
Fill your mouth with exotic fare from foreign lands.

Lie with your lover, caressing breasts and belly.
Guide a lost child across the star-soaked sky.
Hold close the best memories of your life.
Dispose of the blackened corpses.

Acknowledgements

First, I wish to thank Mary K. Wilson for her inspiration, encouragement, and insight as I worked on the poems in this chapbook. She served as first and second reader/listener, making suggestions and corrections, not all of which were, at first, welcomed by the poet, but in the end, were almost always the better choice.

Second, thanks go to all my Waterbean Poetry Night at the Mic friends and fellow poets for providing a welcoming space in which to share early versions of several of these poems. A special thanks goes to Waterbean Poetry founders Jonathan K. Rice and Leslie Rupracht for creating this wonderful venue.

Third, thanks, too, to the editors of *One Minute Magazine* for first publishing "Crowder Peas" and "The Old Main Drag" and to Rusty Barnes and Heather Sullivan at *Live Nude Poems* for first publishing "Corporate Warriors." Also, appreciation goes to the editors of the *2019 Joe Gouveia Outermost Poetry Contest* for awarding an honorable mention to "Upon Learning of the Death of an Old Girlfriend on Facebook before Finishing Your First Cup of Coffee."

Finally, a big thanks to the judges, especially final judge, 2018 Texas Poet Laureate, Carol Coffee Reposa, for selecting this chapbook as the winner of the 2020 Contemporary Poetry Chapbook Prize and to Tony Burnett and his staff at *Kallisto Gaia Press* for bringing it to print.